God must have a sense of humor He made Aardvarks and Orangutans

...and Me!

by David Steele
Illustrated by Marshall Potter

Illuminations Press, St. Helena, California

Library of Congress Catalog Number: 82-084780
ISBN 0-937088-09-9

Manufactured in the United States of America
2 3 4 5 6 7 8 9 10

Books about God seldom smile.
They are serious and solemn and ponderous!

This is a book about God. It is designed to smile.
We need to catch the twinkle in God's eye.

God must have a sense of Humor. God is the Author
of life. All that we have and are come from God.
And that includes humor. It is a gift of Grace.
It is meant to be used . . . at home . . . at work . . .
and (heavens forbid) in church!

We yearn to be close to God. God loves us and seeks us.
Yet we keep God at a distance. How?
The Bible and human experience are clear on this.
It is our human pride that holds God off.
Pride is the ultimate sin.

We manufacture grandiose opinions of ourselves.
We pose; we preen; we strut. We pretend that
we are God Almighty! And this "Godalmightyness"
shuts God out. How sad! How silly!

For we have, right at hand, a rapier that can swiftly
puncture our pride balloons. It is humor;
God's gift to us . . . our finest weapon for
attacking hypocrisy. We use it to laugh at others,
but too infrequently do we laugh at ourselves.
How can God touch us until we do?

An old Jewish proverb states: "When you are hungry,
sing; when you are hurt, laugh." The Rabbis understood
the healing quality of humor. In days of persecution
and suffering they often brought solace to the soul
in torment with a smile.

Modern medicine is rediscovering the therapeutic value
of laughter. We are hearing how humor has been
a servant to healing. Humor is God's gift
to people in distress.

But how hard it has been for Christians to sense
the Grace in humor. Too often we have listened to
the Angel's words: "Behold, I bring you Good News
of Great Joy!" in a solemn, tedious manner.
Our worship is serious business. Too serious!
Blessed is the congregation who has discovered
a smile passing from person to person . . . a chuckle
growing into a communal guffaw . . . and the warmth of
the Good News invading the sanctuary through humor.

We want to touch God. Or better, we want God to touch us.
So we turn to the Bible. It is the source book of Faith.
But it is so hard . . . so solemn!

We talk about "serious Bible study."
And that's what our study is . . . terribly serious.
Groups of earnest Christians sit on straight-backed
chairs; frowns touch their knitted brows; pious words
cross their tight lips—that is Bible study.
It is seldom much fun.

What if we learned to read the Bible
with a sense of humor? Do we dare approach THE WORD
in a lighthearted way? It may be that God's gift
of humor could be the key that will help us relax
with The Book. We might discover all sorts of things we
have missed in our "serious" study. It is worth a try.

The passages that follow have a theme. They are about
the minor events and characters in the Bible.
Here are people like us. Read each passage
of scripture with your sense of humor showing.
Try to picture yourself in the situation and sense
how you would feel.

The meditations are my own response to the passage.
As you read them allow the chuckles to come and groan
at the terrible puns. If some insight strikes, return
to the Bible, see it again in the text.
Allow some time for God's Spirit to touch you.

The approach we are taking is lighthearted but not
lightheaded. It intends to make Bible reading fun
but does not make fun of the reading nor make it funny.
We are simply taking hold of God's gift of humor
to open up the Word. A person sometimes sees
more clearly with a twinkle in the eye.

Leo Rosten defines humor as
"The affectionate communication of insight."
God grant you may find it so.

David Steele,
San Rafael, California

Contents

Let The Children Come
Mark 10:13-16

There's nothing so nice as some children.
Every family should have one or two.,
They are such a fine race
When they're kept in their place,
Say . . . the nursery, the park, or the zoo.

In his place a young child is delightful,
Full of fun, a most int'resting buddy;
But her yearning for action
Can cause a distraction,
When she has invaded the study.

The office is no place for children.
They foul up our work with their fun.
So we make it a rule
That they must go to school
So their elders can get something done.

Some children came searching for Jesus.
His friends were distressed . . . and inclined
To think t'would be terrible
To have a fresh parable
Suddenly slip from his mind.

So they tried to get rid of the children;
Surely no major disgrace,
Protecting their master
From some great disaster,
By keeping the children in place.

Let The Children Come

"Let those children in," Jesus shouted,
And said something frightfully odd.
"They are bearers of Grace,
And their ultimate place
Is right smack in the Kingdom of God."

So . . . the place of a child is the kingdom!
That's what He so carefully taught.
So . . . the last time you did
Play some ball with your kid,
You were closer to God than you thought.

Shiloah
Isaiah 8:6-8

We live "Las Vegas" lives.
Our attention is caught by the big,
the brassy, the spectacular.
The splashy events of life dominate the media.
We assume the big events of life are the important ones.
So when we come to the Bible
we tend to focus our attention ‿
on the highly dramatic passages.

Isaiah spoke about people
whose attention was so completely riveted
upon raging rivers that they missed
the significance of a quiet pool.
By the pool Shiloah he found great personal meaning.
He spoke of the God he had encountered
in quietness . . . on ordinary days . . .
in the midst of the commonplace.

People involved in unusual capers
Get their names in the daily papers;
And people who do unusual things—
Movie stars, congressmen, shortstops, and kings.
Tales of the Great and the Weird have narration,
Especially those which may cause titillation.
Whichever the views I choose to peruse,
The unusual usually rules in the news.

And I scan the papers
    But seldom see
Anyone there
    Who resembles me.

Shiloah

People who've made a particular hit
Tend to be featured in Holy Writ.
Scripture is filled with unusual tales.
People fight giants or orgy with Baals . . .
Water is walked on . . . Bushes keep burning . . .
This is the stuff of my Sunday School learning.
And my usual thought is that usually I'm liable
To find the unusual there in my Bible.

And I search the Bible
 But seldom see
Anyone there
 Who resembles me.

Isaiah spoke of a quiet pool
Whose waters sparkled clear and cool.
He paused for a drink at this spring serene
As a usual part of his daily routine.
Shiloah, he called this pleasant spring
And there he learned an important thing:
"Here," said he, "I find God's grace
Can permeate the commonplace".

We tend to comb life's Grand Events
For signs of God's omnipotence.
And so we feature the unus-
ual in Bibles and in news.
But meanwhile God's Shiloah hand
Is touching things we understand.
When meeting God, I note he hath
Approached me on the beaten path.

And I search the Bible
 At last I see
People there
 Who resemble me!

The Bible

The Sunday School where I was taught
Informed my friends and me we ought
To be completely overawed
When coming near the Word of God.

We learned Good Christian folk were liable
To venerate the Holy Bible.
Our teachers flew into a rage
If dirty hand smudged Holy Page.
And so our fearful fingers shook
When we approached the Holy Book.

We all believed the Rock of Ages
Had placed His Words upon those pages,
And felt that God might strike us dead
If we made fun of what he said.
And so we read the Bible plots
As lots and lots of sober thoughts.
The humorous could never fit
My childhood view of Holy Writ.

But now, not wishing to seem rude,
I must deplore that attitude,
And raise my voice a bit to say
That I have found a better way.

I've found of late that I will tend
To view the Bible as my friend.
An older friend . . . still in his prime
Whose thoughts have stood the test of time.

A friend who'll preach and plead and prod
To lead me in the will of God;
And yet like any counselor
Has small talk in his repertoire.

The Bible

As any friend he will relate
Minutiae that is out of date;
And does not seem to mind the gaffe
Which brings a chuckle or a laugh.

I find that I have really found
A friend, when I can kid around.
That book upon my Bible shelf
Joins me in laughing at myself.

So I have found a friendly sage
On each and every Bible page.
At whom I marvel . . . whom I doubt . . .
I laugh with him, and cry, and shout
Of all the things I find absurd!
And that's the way I hear God's Word.

John The Baptist
John 3:25-30

Jerusalem's most highly famed,
And the aptest
Preacher was quite fitly named
John the Baptist.

He urged repentance long and loud
(And made some cry).
That kind of preaching draws a crowd.
I don't know why.

His charismatic pleading way
Knew no rival.
Before long he was leading a
Great revival.

People came from far and near—
The strong, the weak.
'Twas quite a privilege to hear
This prophet speak.

His fame throughout the countryside
Gave John a lift.
Clerics often find that Pride
Goes with their gift.

Preachers find it rather nice,
As you may note,
Being asked for their advice
Or for a quote.

When one has found his thoughts and views
Have great appeal,
Then starts to notice empty pews;
How does she feel?

John realized his own career
Had passed its peak.
For now the crowds were off to hear
His cousin speak.

John the Baptist

John watched the dwindling attendance
And shook his head.
Of Jesus' rivaling ascendance
These words he said:

"He must INCREASE
I must DECREASE!"

That's not the way most preachers talk.
When in a jam
Does Oral Roberts send his flock
To Billy Graham?

John's ego has been verified.
Large was its place.
This man of pride still stepped aside
With humble grace.

Jesus spoke about John's worth.
We read later:
"Of all the preachers on the earth
None was greater."

Jethro
Exodus 18:1-27

Now I imagine few of us
Would care to lead an Exodus.
For who among us really craves
To lead a horde of former slaves
With all their problems, hopes, and fears
A-wandering for forty years?

Directing an emerging nation
Is a prophetable occupation,
And he who takes the job will be
Assured a place in history.
He'll have no little claim to fame;
Most everyone will know his name.
Prestige, at first, will seem quite nice;
But then, he'll have to pay the price.

Moses did not want to grip
The lonely role of leadership,
But God, one brilliant desert dawn,
Commanded him to take it on;
And feeling he could ill afford
To disobey His Living Lord,
He acquiesced to His request
And gave the job his very best.

No enterprise will long survive
Whose leader works from 9 to 5.
So Moses, being in his prime,
Began to work some overtime.
His office soon became the site
Of meetings nearly every night.
And then he'd take a healthy tome
Of paper work to do at home.
It wasn't long before he'd scoff
At any thought of taking off.
With so much work that must be done
He hadn't time for play or fun,
Nor could he laugh, relax, or frolic.
Moses was a work-a-holic.

Jethro

Now men with hefty power drives
Are seldom heroes to their wives.
The man who leads a busy life
Has little time for home or wife.
Spouses do not have a yen
To join in praising famous men.
They give success a cool reception
And Zipporah was no exception.

The placid Moses whom she married,
Was tired, edgy, tense and harried.
And she suspected he was very
Ready for a coronary.
And so, she felt, 'twas time she had
A little chat with Mom and Dad.

She journeyed, where her parents dwelt
And told her folks just how she felt.
"I didn't want a bed of roses
When I agreed to marry Moses.
I know it takes a lot of gall
To argue with a Holy Call:
But Moses, as you clearly see,
Has time for God . . . but not for me.
I cry myself to sleep at night.
Tell me . . . do you think that's right?"

It caused those parents great distress
To see their child's unhappiness.
And Jethro, dear Zipporah's dad,
Was more than just a trifle mad.
"The time," he thought, "is overdue
To teach that boy a thing or two."

Jethro

Jethro's temper rankled raw
As he sought his son-in-law.
But then he saw, to his dismay,
How Moses spent the working day.
People came from far and near
In hopes of catching Moses' ear.
No problem was too small to mention.
They brought them all to his attention.
The sheer amount of people who
Were waiting for an interview
Caused Jethro to feel rather dizzy.
"My son-in-law is much too busy!
I think I'll play a bit of cupid.
That boy's not bad . . . He's simply stupid."

And so, I'm happy to relate,
Jethro told it to him straight.
"Whoever said you were commanded
To run this country single-handed?
You know you're just the protege
Of God . . . Who rests the seventh day.
Why you've become (That's very odd.)
More indispensible than God.
This schedule you are keeping will
Put you to bed in Ulcerville,
And that's a price we can't afford.
So get some help! Thus saith the Lord!"

Under Jethro's gentle nudges
Moses chose some able judges,
And discovered to his glee
They did the job as well as he.

There's ample help for any task
Once we have the sense to ask!

The Sons of The Prophets
Isaiah 7:3, 8:1-4

Some of us have had the chance
Of growing up inside a manse.
We got advice that then seemed ample
On how to set a good example.
We squirmed inside our Sunday suit
When dad related something cute
That we had thought or said or done,
To illustrate point number one.

We loved our folks, and they loved us;
So we didn't make a lot of fuss.
Although we wished they were less dense
When it came to common sense.
We wished they saw how we were squirmin'
When we heard mentioned in the sermon
Some little thing we say or do
That illustrates point number two.

Many a normal person did
Grow up as a preacher's kid.
And we can think of nothing that
Distinguished us from Mon. through Sat.
But Sunday seemed to be the day
Our private lives were on display,
For one could almost guarantee
We'd illustrate point number three.

The life we lived within the manse
Might have its minor irritants,
Yet most of us were happy creatures
While growing up with all those preachers.
Our lives were really rather mild
When compared to a prophet's child.
Those prophet kids faced quite a chore
And let this be point number four.

The Sons of The Prophets

To illustrate, let us begin
With the names those prophets gave their kin.
Can you imagine how kids would razz
A chap named Maher-shal-al-hash-baz?
A boy would surely play the fool
Who bore that name through grammar school.
But Isaiah, man of fame,
Gave his child that frightful name.

He thought, "To keep God's message fresh
I'll wrap it up in human flesh.
Now when my boy comes in the room
Folk will hear God's word of doom.
Through him the Lord will have his say
'The Spoil is speeding . . . Hasten prey'"
And so his other son, we learn,
He called "A Remnant Shall Return".

Those days a prophet who was "in"
Wrapped his message up in skin.
Hosea's children also bore
Their father's thoughts on peace and war.
On prophet children we have dealt
Because I wonder how they felt.
I doubt they greeted with elation
Life as a sermon illustration.

When one is worried about doomin'
He hasn't time for being human.
I hope each prophet chose to live
With someone much more sensitive.
While they confronted storm and strife,
Perhaps an understanding wife
Renamed each little tad and tike,
And called them Bill or Sue or Mike.

David and Goliath
I Samuel 17:1-11, 38-50

I've noticed we tend to create quite a fuss
Over folks who seem bigger and better than us.
For the world is so vast! Its problems appall!
And our own minds and muscles seem puny and small.
So if someone of stature appears, who declares
He is perfectly willing to run our affairs;
And if we sense his presence is solid and large,
We are simply delighted to put him in charge.

Warfare's a prelude to power and wealth.
But for those in the ranks it is harmful to health
And no one, I guess, is especially thrilled
By the thought that tomorrow he might well be killed.
No wonder those Philistines rested their fate
In the hands of Goliath, who stood 6ft. 8
And weighed 265, whom none could subdue
In hand to hand combat!—Of course, wouldn't you?

Those Philistine warriors drew deep satisfaction
From watching Goliath just itching for action.
Ah, the bliss of the saint comes alike to the sinner
Who senses her money is backing a winner.
Out stepped that giant: "Come fight, he who dares!"
The soldiers of Saul knew the next move was theirs.
What an honor to silence that infidel's sneers!
But no one stepped forth—there were no volunteers.

Once mighty King Saul was troubled and glum. It
Appeared he had no one to send to that summit.
"Some person out there in my timorous clan
Must be a fighter! Go find me that man!"
Off went his minions. (They weren't very sharp.)
They returned with a youth who played beautiful harp.
"Egad," quoth the king, "What an awful position!
I ask for a man, and I get a musician."

David and Goliath

When you're dealt a weak hand the decision is tough.
Of course you can fold, but perhaps you could bluff.
Saul studied that shepherd. He looked mighty plucky.
In the right situation the boy could get lucky.
"I'll go with you, kid. You're my man in this scrimmage.
But of course we must tinker a bit with your image.
My helmet and armor should suitably hide
The scrawny young teen-ager dwelling inside."

On went the armor. The results were trés droll.
Young David appeared in his new warrior-role
Looking fearsome and macho—Oh, you would approve.
But, with all of that weight the poor kid couldn't move.
"I'm sorry, your highness, but as you can see
This clap-trap is useless. It just isn't me.
Your instinct seemed sound, but I tell you, O King,
I am much better off with some stones and my sling."

Well, you know the rest. Goliath was slain.
It was David who cruised into victory lane.
And is there a moral? Well, one might be honed.
You see the results when Goliath got stoned.
But I think that this passage comes close to exposing
The folly of all of our post'ring and posing.
The tasks we are given will yield with less fuss
When we use the equipment that's suited to us.

Christmas Eve
Luke 2:1-14

We place the precious Christmas manger
Upon the mantle . . . out of danger.
Hand-painted Kings from Hummel lands
Are putty in young, chubby hands;
And glass-blown sheep are too exquisite
And fragile for a child to visit.
So, while we like them very much,
We ask the kids to look . . . DON'T TOUCH!

But once, I saw on a low table,
Mary, Joseph, star and stable,
The Babe, some sheep, and several kings . . .
Heavy, sturdy, rough-hewn things.
Here children dawdled—took their ease,
Read the sign: "Come, touch us, please."
And every child produced a fresh
Arrangement of that Christmas Creche.

While donkeys watched the Baby sleep,
Angels petted woolly sheep.
And Mary rested from the noise
As Joseph chatted with the boys.
Each child knew to some degree
Just how that scene was meant to be.
I watched, with quite a little mirth
Them orchestrate the Holy Birth.

So God, for her who understands,
Entrusts His coming to our hands.
He urges us now to begin
To place ourselves, our kith and kin . . .
And choose, among the many choices,
Where best we'll hear those angels' voices;
And join that Hallelujah Chorus
Knowing God's at hand . . . and for us.

So, friends, with bright and shiny faces,
The King is coming! Take your places!

Jesus in The Temple
Luke 2:41-51

We wait for what seems a bit more than eternity
For that magical moment of Pa and Ma-ternity.
Prenatal suspense seems to stretch into years.
It provides the occasion for worries and fears.
So when we see our offspring in wrinkled repose,
And it has the right numbers of fingers and toes,
From our hearts comes a prayer that is real, if informal,
"Thank God that our baby is healthy and normal."

Now normal is nice—but that term is too mild
To describe the uniqueness we see in our child.
For each set of parents knows perfectly well
That their own little tyke will achieve and excel;
And each word or action is carefully sifted
For signs that their darling is specially gifted.
Why, those children are ours! We know by all means
There is genius embedded down thar in them genes.

We've read the account in the paper, I guess,
'Bout the five-year old boy playing masterful chess;
Or the girl who at six basks in critical praise
After flawlessly playing Chopin's Polonaise.
But we search high and low for some signal that our
Own budding genius is starting to flower.
But she's stuck in a classroom with some nincompoop
Who insists she can't handle the top reading group.

So it's easy to sense the parental elation
That Mary and Joseph felt on their vacation.
The big city tour was essentially done
When these parents lost track of their 12-year old son.
I guess they were frantic, perhaps even wild,
As they tried to uncover some trace of their child.
They turned to the Temple for guidance and prayer,
And to their amazement young Jesus was there.

Jesus in The Temple

Where the scholars had gathered to pontificate
And engage one another in heady debate,
There in their midst sat this pre-adolescent
With a light in his eyes that was nigh incandescent.
His questions revealed a superb intellect
And were treated with deep academic respect.
That young couple perceived that, at last, they had run
Onto signs that they had a quite talented son.

I suppose that those parents, as other folks do,
Toyed with sending their boy to Jerusalem U.
It appeared he could easily garner permission
To matriculate soon with an early admission.
Their dreams of his future become crystal clear.
A quick Ph.D.—then a brilliant career.
Or maybe he ought to try preaching awhile
For a good teenage guru is always in style.

When a child shows some genius—here are the results:
He is pushed into rigors more fit for adults.
And the pressure applied is the reason that plenty
Of prodigies burn out before they are twenty.
Thank God this temptation was duly resisted
By Mary and Joseph, who wisely insisted
That Jesus come home, as they certainly did,
And grow up in their house like a regular kid.

That's why, when at thirty, on that crucial day
That he started to preach, Christ had something to say.

The Man With One Talent
Matthew 25:14-30

Jesus, tell me why'd you choose
   To fire such a cannon . . . ade
At that poor chap who wouldn't use
His talent, cause he was afraid?
I think your point is very fitting
   When many talents I com . . . mand;
But not when I find myself sitting
With a single talent in my hand.
For I find your admonition to be fully involved and daring is a
cinch to follow in areas where I feel competent and smart.
 But not in situations where I have one talent or less, say
something vaguely connected with art. When I try to draw some-
 thing I freeze up, my golden touch becomes dross. I can't
even draw eight straight lines and come up with a presentable cross . . .

If ever I must draw a cross
I draw a blank instead.
 I am completely at a loss
And want to hide my head.
At such times I can't be eager.
 There is nothing satisfying
When my talent is so meager.
What's the use of even trying?
Jesus, you might show more grace
 Toward people who don't try
 Had you encountered face to face
 A fearsome cross, as I.

But, of course, you did . . . forgive me Lord!

Well, back to the old
drawing board!

Methuselah
Genesis 5:25-27

I'll be danged if I thought
That I ever would see
The day when my picture
Would be on T.V.
Oh, I s'pose that I've lived
A pretty good life,
Raised some mighty fine kids
With my wonderful wife.
And I 'spect if you ask
You'll find they all say
That I give a day's work
When I get a day's pay.
I lived pretty good;
Course, I didn't get fat;
But I never was famous
Or nothin' like that.
And most of my life
Seems no one much cares
'Bout my opinions
On Current Affairs.

So I'm livin' along
Like a plain citizen
When them papers found out
I'm a hundred and ten.
Well, you should have saw
All the fuss they all made.
Course, I 'spect that you did
If you watched the parade.
Did you see the new roadster
Just ahead of the band?
Well, I'm the Old Geezer
Who was wavin' his hand.

Methuselah

Now I never have been
A right hard-hearted cuss,
So I have to admit
I enjoyed all the fuss.
And I got a real kick
When them newspaper guys
Was askin' me questions
Just like I was wise.
They give me that nickname
You heard around town.
So now you are talkin'
To Methuselah Brown.
They're callin' me that
Cause I guess it appears
I may live nine hundred
And sixty-nine years.

When I was a boy
I remarked to my pa
That I'd like to live
Long as old Methuselah.
Course, I know some things now
That I didn't know then.
Your perspective gets changed
At a hundred and ten.

Now in my time
I've had lots of adventures,
But I don't want eight hundred,
More years with these dentures.
With eyes almost shot
And persnickity ears
Who wants to be livin'
For hundreds of years?

Methuselah

I told them reporters
I thought they was wrong
To think I done somethin'
Just by livin' so long.
When a fella like me
Takes so long to depart,
That don't necessarily
Mean that he's smart.
But they write on them pads
Every word that I speak.
At a hundred and ten
I've become quite a freak.
And I guess that they'll put me
(At least till I die)
On public display
Every 4th of July.

You'll see me next year
As we pass the grandstand.
I'm the Old Geezer
Still wavin' his hand.

Aarondipity
Exodus 17:8-13

Folk encounter fresh demands
When setting off for Promised Lands.
The freedom road for slave or serf
Soon leads across another's turf.
Established types don't want their daughters
Entertained by foreign squatters.
If you savor love and charity
Try not to be a refugee.

And, so when Israel's freedom trek
Came near the lands of Amelek,
The angry, armed Amelekite
Forced the fleeing slaves to fight.
(It doesn't take a lot of brav'ry
To fight when you are facing slav'ry).

Moses, as he was wont to do,
Bit off much more than he could chew.
"Upon this hill I'll stand," he said,
"Holding God's Rod above my head
To show my men they fight this hour
Armed with Godly strength and pow'r".

Now folk may conquer fearful odds
When they believe their cause is God's.
So Israel fought as if inspired
And prevailed . . . till Moses tired.
His worn out muscles could not bear
The Rod of God up in the air,
And as his arms began to droop
So did the spirits of his troop.
Their battle lines began to break
As they perceived the great Mose ache.

Aarondipity

Middle-aged prophets may be prone
To overtax their muscle tone;
They hate to think they've gotten older.
So two friends moved 'neath Moses' shoulder—
Aaron-right and Hur on left
Gave his arms a mighty heft,
And bringing all their strength to bear
Raised Moses' arms high in the air.

Once more Moses on his height
Presented an inspiring sight.
His men knew God would have them free,
And fought to stunning victory.

Humanity oft gives its praise
To charismatic ones who raise
Their arms encouraging the rest
Of us to strive to do our best.

But let us praise a different sort—
The unsung ones who give support.
The one who cares and understands
And helps the Great hold up His hands.
For history gives ample hints
That there's a "propper" behind each prince.

At The Altar
Matthew 5:23-24

This world should
Be a Brotherhood,
On that we may agree;
And my heart melts
For everyone else,
But their hearts don't melt for me.

I never cease
To work for peace
In the human family.
So I get along
With the weak and the strong;
But they don't get along with me.

I love every man
As much as I can
To fulfill Christ's clear command.
But the folk that I see
Who refuse to love me
Are the people I can't stand.

Before the altar
I often falter.
I can't go through the motion.
I have the desire
But my sister's ire
Is spoiling my devotion.

Hasn't she heard
Jesus' clear word
That she's on the road to hell?
Her arrogant role
Is destroying her soul
And my peace of mind as well.

At The Altar

This world's a mess
I must confess;
And it won't be any good
Till God gets my brother,
In some way or other,
To treat me the way that he should.

If you wish to increase
The amount of peace,
Here's a place for you to start.
Put lots of love,
Dear God above,
In the other person's heart.

Eutychus
Acts 20:9-12

Now I suppose that it is fair to speak of worship
  as divine
As long as one takes special care to omit the matter of
  pew design.
There is absolutely nothing divine about sitting in
  your average church pew—
Be it old or be it new.
Every pew has one board that cuts off the circulation
  just behind the knees and another board cutting into
  the small of the back.
That results in a co-efficient of comfort roughly
  equivalent to an hour spent on the rack.
Another of the pew's dubious charms:
There is no place to put your arms.
In fancy churches with foam rubber cushions, be they
  Liberal or Orthodoxix,
You will find an upholstery button caressing your
  coccyx.
Church pews
Are not Good News!

When pew designers sit down at their drawing boards,
  they do not ask, "Will the congregation like us?"
No, they are obsessed with the challenge posed by
  the descendants of Eutychus.
Eutychus was the young man from Troas mentioned in
  Acts 20:9-12,
(If you care to get your Bible off the shelve.)
Who was sitting in an open window, trying to follow
  the theological meanderings of the Apostle Paul,
When he dropped off . . . both to sleep and from the
  ledge . . . undergoing a three story fall.
And when everybody rushed downstairs to see if he
  was soffering,
He asked, in his dazed condition, "Oh, did I miss
  the offering?"

Eutychus

Well, you can see why church leaders, whether they
    are people of poverty or wealth,
Have concluded that sleeping in church may be hazardous
    to your health.
So pew makers have been ordered to build into their
    creations as much discomfort as the average person
    can take,
In hopes that the faithful will stay awake.
But if congregational somnolence is what they wish
    to abort,
I say, teach the preachers to keep it short.

There is a Lad Here . . .
John 6:1-14

I wish I were a hero,
A martyr or a saint,
But so far I'm batting zero
For my life is rather quaint.

I could rage and shout like Amos
Or missionate like Paul,
But the chance of being famous
Hasn't come my way at all.

For the villains who need chiding
Don't live near my address;
Nor do kings who seek confiding,
Nor apostles in distress.

So I'm really getting nervous
That, ahead of me, there ain't
No act of thrilling service
That will make of me a saint.

No, the earth will not be shaken
By an act of mine, not nary.
For unless I am mistaken
I am rather ordinary.

I've come of late to ponder
On something I have read
About that day of wonder
When 5,000 souls were fed.

It seems there was a lad
Among that hungry bunch
Who acted rather mad
When he offered Christ his lunch.

I bet others thought him daft.
I wonder what they said?
I suspect they grinned and laughed
When he gave his fish and bread.

There is a Lad Here . . .

"Five loaves . . . Two fish . . . five thousand folk?
Now that is really dumb!
Will someone tell that crazy bloke
We'll only get a crumb?"

He may have yearned, as I,
To pull off some great big deal,
Move the earth or change the sky
Or produce a catered meal.

In that desert dry and hilly,
The simple country lad,
Feeling 'sorta' silly,
Offered Jesus what he had.

But what he had was plenty.
Jesus took his fish and bread;
With it not ten or twenty,
But five thousand folk were fed.

From this I've come to understand
What cannot be denied:
A little gift in Jesus' hand
Is vastly multiplied.

Oh, I'll lead no great invasion
Of that I have a hunch;
But there may be an occasion
When I can share my lunch.

'Tis time for me to cease to rant
About the race I never ran,
And all I want to do but can't,
And do the things I can.

'Twould be nice to be a saint
To join the Holy clan;
Yet, I have no real complaint.
It's all right to be a man.

Michal
2 Samuel 6:12-23

Michal was loyal
To everything royal,
For she was the daughter of Saul.
But her husband was poorish
And awfully boorish,
With simply no manners at all.

It was her fate
To marry a mate
Who had grown up with chickens and sheep.
How to bring charm
To this boy from the farm
Was causing his queen to lose sleep.

Oh, she had to confess
He was a success.
In the eyes of the world, Dave was famous.
But of how kings comport
Themselves when in court
He remained a complete ignoramus.

David's heart soared
And he danced to the Lord
In a manner more free than refined.
And his poor little wife
Got the shock of her life;
So she gave him a piece of her mind.

"I don't care a smidgen
About your religion
As long as it's solemn and chaste.
But the way you're behaving
With arms wildly waving
Is shockingly lacking in taste."

Michal

"While I agree dancing
Is fine for romancing,
And I've done no extensive research,
I hope you will see
That it lacks dignity
And is frightfully bad form in church."

"If you must raise
Your spirit in praise,
Please see that it's soothing and calm.
The Lord, I am sure,
Would really prefer
Something more like the 23rd Psalm."

Then God's anointed
Became disappointed.
He knew he had nary a chance
Of ever persuadin'
This prim, regal maiden
That the Lord is a lover of dance.

Churches these days
Talk a lot about Praise
And the Joy that accomp'nies Good News.
But don't tap your feet
Or get out of the seat
For Michal still lurks in the pews.

And when you have ended
She might be offended.
And so, it is better by far
To act out your praise
On those great joyful days
With some friends at a neighborhood bar.

Zaccheaus
Luke 19-1-10

On the brow of a hill,
Near the edge of a wood,
Was the place where the house
Of Zaccheaus stood.
Such a house! Why it looked
Really more like a mansion.
The yard was enormous
With room for expansion
And a large swimming pool
And a neat tennis court.
Why, you'd think you were at
A vacation resort.
Now if you saw that house,
I suspect that you might
Think the owner was rich.
And by golly, you're right!
And you might think as well
That he'd have quite a long
List of friends come to visit
Him. Nope! There you're wrong!

For one thing 'bout Zaccheaus
Just wasn't too pretty.
He collected the taxes,
In Jericho City.
That's how he got rich.
Not from his honest labors,
But by fleecing his friends
And then cheating his neighbors.
Those people agreed that
It just wasn't funny.
"He's built that big mansion
Of his with our money.
So if he acts that way,
We won't even pretend
That we like him at all
Or that he is our friend!"

Zacchaeus

Zacchaeus was wealthy.
He lived well, and only
One thing was amiss.
He was awfully lonely.
For when he came to town
And nodded, "Good Day"
The people around him
Would just turn away.
They showed him their backs
And averted their eyes.
And when he walked on
They made fun of his size.
For Zacchaeus was shorter
Than most other folks,
And shorties are often
The target for jokes.
So often he heard
A quite terrible tease
"Just look at that man
Walking round on his knees!"
His ears would get red
As he heard people snicker;
But he wouldn't look back;
He'd just walk by much quicker.
And he'd think to himself,
"Let them chuckle and roar.
I'll have the last laugh,
I'll just cheat them some more!"

So you can imagine
The fuss people made
That day when Zacchaeus
Came to the parade.
Well, it wasn't one, really,
But it looked like it was.
People crowded the sidewalks
And watched hard, because

Zacchaeus

They all wanted to see
A great man of renown
Named Jesus of Nazareth
Come into town.

They hoped he would teach
Them some things about God.
But when they saw Zacchaeus
They said, "Now, that's odd.
Why would a cheater
So riddled with sin
Want to see Jesus?
We won't let him in!"

They stood on tiptoes
And made themselves tall,
So poor little Zacchaeus
Couldn't get close at all.
Zacchaeus tried hard,
But he just couldn't see.
So you know what he did?
He climbed up in a tree!

You must give him credit.
He surely was spunky.
But his neighbors just snickered,
"Hey, look at the monkey!"
They laughed till they hurt
And some started to cry.
At that very moment
Why, Jesus rode by.
He stopped by that tree
On the outskirts of town
And called in a loud voice,
"Zacchaeus, come down.
I'm tired and I'm hungry
And I just had a hunch
That over at your place
You serve a fine lunch."

Zacchaeus

Well, Zacchaeus hopped down
And he puffed out his chest.
He was proud to have Jesus
As his luncheon guest.
But the people around him
All started to fret.
You could tell at a glance
They were mighty upset.

"Say, we wanted Jesus
To come to our house,
But now he is planning
To eat with that louse!
Zach serves a fine meal.
He's a very good cook,
But, Heavens to Betsy,
That man is a crook!
We just don't believe Jesus,
Who's pious and prim,
Should be messing around
With a person like him!"

But Jesus said, "Posh!
It won't matter whether
People approve. Let's
Go have lunch together."

After they ate, Jesus said,
"Zach, I've found
That you're not the most popular
Person around.
You're selfish and mean
And you cheat people, too.
Why do you suppose
That you act as you do?"

Zacchaeus

"I'd like to be nicer"
Said Zach, "if I could,
But I have to admit
I am really no good.
People don't like me much
When I meet 'em or greet 'em
Since they won't be my friends
Then I might as well cheat 'em."

"That's nonsense, Zacchaeus,"
Said Jesus, "It's bunk!
When God makes a person
He doesn't make junk!
There's a wonderful man
Inside you," said the Savior,
"But you won't let him out
With your dreadful behavior.
Now you could become
That great little guy
Today! If you wanted
To give it a try."

Zacchaeus thought hard.
You could see him decide.
Then he leaped from his chair
And he hurried outside.
There were his neighbors—
The whole angry bunch
Waiting for Jesus
To finish his lunch.

"Friends," said Zacchaeus
"I've gotten quite rich
By cheating you all.
But, now I'm going to switch!
I've been wrong, and I see
I've been very mistaken.
So I'm giving you back
Four times what I have taken.

Zacchaeus

I'm going to be different.
And just to make sure
I'll give half of my money
Away to the poor.
And from now on I'm acting
The way that I should."
Then he started to smile
'Cause he felt pretty good.

He remarked, "Thank you, Jesus
For helping me see
There's a very good person
That really is me."

Well, of course, those folks wondered,
Just like people do,
If all Zach had promised
Would really come true.
But it did! And soon no one
Would ever deny
That Zacchaeus had turned out
To be a nice guy.

And we really should add,
Before this story ends,
That soon old Zacchaeus
Had plenty of friends.
They said, "It is funny
But we think, somehow,
Zach has started to grow;
He seems much bigger now.

But he was still short
Like he's been at the start.
What those people saw now
Was the size of his heart!

Miracles
Matthew 14:22-32

I well recall my Bible class.
We read how Jesus trod the sea.
I often watched the little lass
Who sat two seats away from me.

I noticed she began to draw
In her book, among her notes,
A quite amazing replica
Of Jesus standing on two boats.

I thought, "A soul could not obtain
A statement much more lyrical.
That drawing makes completely plain
Her thoughts about that miracle."

And when we got to talking
She was clear about her views:
If a man goes water walking
He must wear enormous shoes.

She had chosen the empirical
As her daily regimen,
So she asked of every miracle,
"Did that really happen then?"

We haven't met in years.
I wonder what she'd say.
Do you think she still adheres
To that point of view today?

'Cause I have a new suggestion
I am ready to avow
Of a more important question:
"Does that ever happen Now?"

Not long ago I very nearly
Forfeited my poise and balance,
By taking on a task that clearly
Over-stretched my meager talents.

Miracles

I was going well, pursuing
Goals with vigor, vim, and verve.
Till I thought, "What am I doing?"
And began to lose my nerve.

Thoughts of failure, and of dread
Were the ones that I could think.
I was in above my head
And I felt my spirits sink.

I was ready to give in,
(Which is something I despise)
Till a friend began to grin
As I looked into his eyes.

The message there was plain.
I could see that it was true:
"Stop acting so inane,
For I still believe in you."

That gave me such a lift!
I'm so grateful to that man!
For I made a major shift
From "I Cannot" to "I Can".

I finished simply great.
O, success was never sweeter.
And soon I could relate
My experience with Peter.

The way that Jesus reached to save
Floundering Peter in that sea.
And kept his head above the wave,
Was what my friend had done for me.

I was joyful and elated,
More than just a trifle awed.
Had I just participated
In a miracle of God?

Miracles

·I still have not decided
What took place in Peter's boat.
But I know the Lord provided
Strength to keep my head afloat.

I think that I could show
My friend . . . If we should ever meet,
That to traipse on H_2O
You don't need gigantic feet.

Has living also taught her
(I have a hunch it may)
That walking on the water
Is quite commonplace today?

Paul and Barnabas
Acts 15:36-41

Human beings should act moral!
With that we do not choose to quarrel.
Yet, most of us have had a session
With, what we termed, an indiscretion;
And found, sometimes to our chagrin,
We quite enjoyed our touch of sin.

We do not choose, nor would we dare,
To make of sin our daily fare.
And while, at times, we've smiled or quipped
On learning that our neighbor slipped,
We tend to be quite tolerant.
For we have learned that humans can't
Be perfect in the task of living;
So it is best to be forgiving.

While most of us walk more or less
Along the paths of righteousness,
A few folk simply won't pollute
Their systems with forbidden fruit.
They look like us, but seem to feel
A special sort of moral zeal,
And find an almost strange delight
In knowing they are doing right.
They live their lives without a flaw
Keeping the letter of the law.
And one might think that they, perhaps,
Have never had a moral lapse.
With folk like this, for heaven's sake,
Don't even make a small mistake;
For you will find to your regret
They can't forgive and won't forget.

When Paul was Saul we know that he
Was trained to be a Pharisee.
He learned in pharisaic fashion
To love the law with firey passion
And felt a mission to imprison
Those with different views from his'n.

Paul and Barnabas

When Paul came to his colossal
Appointment as Christ's chief apostle,
His former life was rearranged.
In many ways the man was changed.
But naught on that Damascus Road
Affected Paul's high moral code.
While he, in theory, might embrace
That we are justified by Grace,
His youthful legalistic ways
Were more than just a passing phase.

Paul felt that Christians should approach
Behavior that's above reproach.
His moral views were quite demanding!
He hadn't lots of understanding
For those who slipped . . . Tho he might try.
Paul was a quite judgmental guy.

So that's the context of the fuss
That came 'twixt Paul and Barnabas,
When they were starting to equip
Their second missionary trip.

Barney wanted Mark to go.
And Paul replied an angry, "No!"
He pointed out with frosty frown
How Mark had let the mission down
When he abandoned his fair share
And disappeared to . . . God knows where.

"I'll not attempt," th'apostle glowered,
"Another journey with that coward!"

Barnabas insisted, "Paul,
That bright young man's received God's Call.
I know last time he lost his nerve,
But now he really wants to serve.
Don't turn your back without a glance!
That boy deserves a second chance!"

Paul and Barnabas

When Paul took stands, we do not find
He very often changed his mind.
And he was sure it wasn't right
To trust that tarnished neophyte.
In this Paul stood quite resolute!
(Forgiveness wasn't his strong suit.)

This quarrel raised a dreadful wall
Between good Barnabas and Paul.
So much, in fact, they doubted whether
They ought to try to work together.

So Paul, at last, was quite insistent
That he would take a new assistant.
While Barney and his protege
Could serve the Lord their own sweet way.

Paul was firm and quite unbending.
And yet there was a happy ending.
As Barnabas believed he must,
The young Mark blossomed in his trust.
Mark brought the cause of Christ acclaim.
And wrote the book that bears his name.
His service had such great effect
He even garnered Paul's respect.

'Tis fitting that we all confess
The limits to our righteousness.
For, like Paul, you know we might
Be doing wrong, by being right.

Communion
1 Corinthians 11:23-26

This table now is simply spread
With little loaves of common bread . . .
Not pumpernickel, corn, or rye
To spark the taste or please the eye . . .
Just bread . . . It's sold in any store.
I've had it many times before.

I am accustomed, when a guest,
To being rather more impressed.
I might expect a gracious host
To brown the bread and make some toast,
Or see his table was arrayed
With butter, jam, and marmalade.
Danish pastries filled with jam,
Some scrambled eggs with lots of ham.
This would impress me more. Instead,
The Lord shares common, daily bread.

I'll eat this bread; but I will find
Its taste won't linger in my mind.
This bread is easy to dismiss.
I've had ten thousand bites like this.
This bread, I think, in many ways
Reminds me of my common days.

Some days are vivid in design,
Resembling an exotic wine . . .
Days of joy and days of sorrow.
(One may well arrive tomorrow.)

But nearly all the days I've led
Are more like this plain, common bread;
Like, say, last 19th of September.
(A day I simply can't remember.)
It's gone . . . slipped from my memory
Just as this bread is bound to be.

Communion

At this table I shall praise
The God who gives me common days.
And I shall live these days with pride,
Knowing God moves by my side.
For at this table God has said:
"I share with you this daily bread"
And by this Word we all are fed.

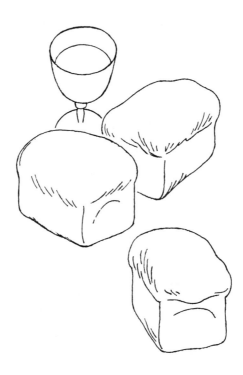

The Lucky Soldier
John 19:23-25

Honey, give your hair a comb;
Your soldier boy is fin'lly home.
Put on your brightest, finest gown,
Cause we are gonna paint the town.
Tonight we sing and dance and play,
For this has been my lucky day!

Shade your eyes against the glare
And look at what I'm gonna wear!
Here's the robe in which I'll dine.
Don't it look fine? And now it's mine!
Yes, mine! That's what you heard me say.
Today has been my lucky day!

You know it would have taken ages
To buy this on my paltry wages.
Such workmanship! It seems to gleam!
Just see if you can find the seam!
You can't? Of course, there isn't any.
This must have cost a pretty penny.

Now, don't start any argument.
This didn't cost a blessed cent.
I got it from that strange buffoon
We crucified this afternoon.
His need for it was gone and done.
We threw the lots . . . And look who won!

God knows, I've taken many losses,
Gambling there among those crosses.
Perhaps my stars are rearranged.
I guess my luck has really changed.
This robe would go for three months pay!
Today is sure my lucky day!

Fetch that calendar, dear mate,
And let me mark this lovely date.
Good Friday's what I'm gonna call it.
It won't matter if I scrawl it,
'Cause I'll remember, anyway,
What happened on my lucky day!

The Temple Veil
Matthew 27:51

We've come to call God's Friday, "Good".
I'm not at all convinced we should.
It may be just a cover up
To justify that bitter cup.

If "good" means we ignore the tragic
By using clever verbal magic
And miss the sheer insanity
Of mankind's inhumanity,
Then we should find a better name
To designate that day of shame.

Yet, one event that horrid day
Was very good in every way.
As Matthew tells the ancient tale,
It seems God tore the Temple veil—
Which acted as a kind of proof
That God preferred to stay aloof—
And by this act of daring grace,
God left his sheltered Holy Place
And let us know God had a yen
To be involved with sinful men.

In ages past, as you may note,
God dwelt apart and quite remote
Upon a High and Holy Place.
Man dared not look upon God's face.

And when men sought the Lord's advice
Through ritual and sacrifice,
Why, nearly everybody tried
To act grown up and dignified.
God was straight, and rather stuffy;
And little 'goofs' could make God huffy.

The Temple Veil

Now children bring some strange results
To over-dignified adults.
One cannot choose to be aloof
When little ones live 'neath the roof.
All parents know a child soon teaches
The joys of playgrounds, zoos, and beaches . . .
How to laugh and have some fun . . .
And sure enough, before she's done,
A child weans her parental buddies
Far away from stuffy studies.

So it appears, the Holy One
Was quite affected by His Son,
Who coaxed God, as we might have known,
To leave God's lofty, heav'nly throne
And walk at eve in Galilee
Smelling the breeze from off the sea.
Jesus showed his Dad the worth
Of all the wonders of this earth.
They watched the sun rise in the east;
Enjoyed a happy wedding feast;
Helped a farmer sow his seed;
And shared concern for men in need.

God saw His world through Jesus' eyes
And dropped the lofty, royal guise.
God ripped the Holy Veil aside
To be with us . . . when Jesus died.

Call to Worship
Psalm 150

PRAISE THE LORD!

We never were intended, surely,
To come to church so doggoned early.
Yet, here I am beneath this steeple
Gathered with God's dozin' people.
Just look at us! . . . I might have guessed . . .
We all could use a lot more rest.
Perhaps this morn we'll be so blessed.

PRAISE GOD IN HIS SANCTUARY!
PRAISE HIM IN HIS MIGHTY FIRMAMENT!

Good! . . . He's going to read a psalm.
I love them, for they seem so calm.
I'll join the other people here
And let my mind slip out of gear.

PRAISE HIM FOR HIS MIGHTY DEEDS!
PRAISE HIM ACCORDING TO HIS EXCEEDING GREATNESS!

The Smiths are late . . . They'll have to wait.
(My word, it's hard to concentrate!)

PRAISE HIM WITH TRUMPET SOUND!

I've come to find some peace and ease;
And so, Dear Lord, no trumpets, please!
Well, I recall, that dreadful noise
Committed by those Beazley boys
Who tooted here last Eastertide
And gave me thoughts of homicide.

PRAISE HIM WITH LUTE AND HARP!

Lutes and Harps . . . That's much more wise!
And I'll lean back and close my eyes . . .

Call to Worship

PRAISE HIM WITH TIMBREL AND DANCE!

Do you suppose there's any chance
That someone will get up and dance?
Oh, no one here would be so crass!
Thank God, we're upper middle class!

PRAISE HIM WITH STRINGS AND PIPE!
PRAISE HIM WITH SOUNDING CYMBALS!

What?

PRAISE HIM WITH SOUNDING CYMBALS! (CRASH!)

One more like that, for heaven's sake,
And we will all be wide awake.

PRAISE HIM WITH LOUD CRASHING CYMBALS! (CRASH! CRASH

Well, Lord, I guess to each one here
Your point is now completely clear.
You seem to feel your drowsy sheep
Can't worship well while half asleep.
We thought you were more tenderhearted.
But now we're up . . . So let's get started!

LET EVERYTHING THAT BREATHES PRAISE THE LORD!
PRAISE THE LORD!